Acting:
Stage & Screen

ART TODAY!

Acting: Stage & Screen

Art Festivals & Galleries:
The Art of Selling Art

Comedy & Comedians

Filmmaking & Documentaries

Music & Musicians

Painting

Performing Arts

Photography

Sculpting

Writing: Stories, Poetry, Song, & Rap

Acting:
Stage & Screen

Z.B. Hill

Mason Crest

Mason Crest
450 Parkway Drive, Suite D
Broomall, PA 19008
www.masoncrest.com

Printed and bound in the United States of America.

First printing
9 8 7 6 5 4 3 2 1

Series ISBN: 978-1-4222-3167-8
ISBN: 978-1-4222-3168-5
ebook ISBN: 978-1-4222-8705-7

Library of Congress Cataloging-in-Publication Data

Hill, Z. B.
  Acting : stage and screen / Z.B. Hill.
      pages cm. — (Art today!)
  Includes bibliographical references and index.
  ISBN 978-1-4222-3168-5 (hardback : alk. paper) — ISBN 978-1-4222-3167-8 (series : alk. paper) — ISBN 978-1-4222-8705-7 (ebook)
  I. Title.
  PN2061.H56 2014
  792.02'8—dc23
                                        2014011825

Contents

1. Acting on Stage and Screen   7

2. The History of Acting on Stage and Screen   19

3. The Business of Acting on Stage and Screen   31

4. How Can I Get Involved in Acting?   45

Find Out More   59

Series Glossary of Key Terms   61

Index   62

About the Author & Picture Credits   64

KEY ICONS TO LOOK FOR:

Text-Dependent Questions: These questions send the reader back to the text for more careful attention to the evidence presented there.

Words to Understand: These words with their easy-to-understand definitions will increase the reader's understanding of the text, while building vocabulary skills.

Series Glossary of Key Terms: This back-of-the book glossary contains terminology used throughout this series. Words found here increase the reader's ability to read and comprehend higher-level books and articles in this field.

Research Projects: Readers are pointed toward areas of further inquiry connected to each chapter. Suggestions are provided for projects that encourage deeper research and analysis.

Sidebars: This boxed material within the main text allows readers to build knowledge, gain insights, explore possibilities, and broaden their perspectives by weaving together additional information to provide realistic and holistic perspectives.

Words to Understand

medium: The way or means by which something is done.

standing ovation: When an audience stands at the end of a performance to show their appreciation.

professional: Doing something for a living, and usually being very good at it.

royalty: A sum of money paid to an author or composer for each copy of a book sold or for each public performance of a work.

musical: A play where much of the dialogue and action is shown through singing songs.

comedy: A play filled with jokes, designed to get the audience to laugh.

drama: An exciting or emotional genre of performances.

props: Objects other than furniture that you use during a performance.

project: To push your voice out loudly without shouting, so that it fills a large space.

sequentially: In order.

Chapter One

Acting on Stage and Screen

You and some friends are at the movies, watching a blockbuster starring your favorite actor. She seems to be able to play any kind of character. Her last hit was a romantic comedy. This time, she is an alien in a science fiction film. And while you know much of the action is computer generated, it is still fun to watch her battle humans. You think to yourself: *It must be fun to be able to be different kinds of people. At least for a little while. I'd love to dress up and become someone else. And having superpowers would be all right, too.*

A few nights later, you and your family are at the theater to see a play. It is your first play, and you are not quite sure what to expect. After a while, you are completely caught up in what is happening onstage. It seems so real. You have seen the actors on television and in the movies, but never right in front of you. But the truth is, you really do

Make Connections

Originally, the word "actor" referred to both males and females. Later, women became known as "actresses." In the mid-1950s, "actor" again came to be used to refer to both males and females. Today, the term "actress" is usually used only in names of awards.

not remember those other performances as you watch the actors in the play. In fact, they have become the people they are playing. You think to yourself: *These actors are really good. I can really see them as the characters they are playing. It must take a lot of talent to be an actor and to get the audience to believe you are someone else.*

If you want to be an actor, you have many options. You can act on the stage, in a movie, or on television. And though you may want to go to Hollywood, New York City, or some other location known for acting opportunities, you can find them much closer to home.

No matter where you perform or in what **medium**, acting means you temporarily become someone else and entertain others. How you do that varies between stage and screen.

PERFORMING ONSTAGE

When you act onstage—in a theater—you provide your audience with an experience they cannot obtain elsewhere. Audience members watch you perform live, on the spot. There is no time delay and no editing out mistakes.

As for you as an actor, you do not have to wait for ratings to learn

Make Connections

Famous actor Paul Newman said, "Acting is a question of absorbing other people's personalities and adding some of your own experience."

how people liked your performance or the play. If your character said something funny and the audience did not laugh, you immediately know there could be a problem. Maybe it was how you delivered—said—your line. Or maybe the line or situation was not funny. On the other hand, if they laughed, you know you got it right. And after the performance, thunderous applause or even a *standing ovation* lets you know you did a good job. But a smattering of polite applause could mean a short run or even opening and closing on the same night.

Most productions run for more than one night. School plays may run for a weekend or two. Community theaters usually schedule multiple performances. *Professional* theater companies can perform a play for months, if not years. So keep in mind that though performance mistakes can be obvious when they happen, you will likely have the opportunity to fix them quickly.

FAMILIARITY:
THE GOOD AND THE INTIMIDATING

A playwright is someone who writes plays. Once the play is written, it is generally published. After a play is published, any theater group can put it on, often after paying a *royalty* to the publishing company. The play can then be studied in school as part of English, literature, or

William Shakespeare, probably the most famous playwright who ever lived, was also an actor.

Make Connections

Outstanding Broadway performances are recognized by the American Theatre Wing's Tony Awards®. The youngest winner of a Tony was Frankie Michaels, who played Patrick Dennis in *Mame*. He won the 1966 Best Featured Actor in a Musical award a month after he turned eleven.

theater classes. If the playwright is lucky—and the play is good—it can become as well known and appreciated as such classics as those by William Shakespeare, Harold Pinter, Edward Albee, and other famous playwrights.

What does that have to do with being an actor? When someone plays a character onstage, it is likely many others have played that character as well, especially if it is a successful play. There may even be others playing the character at the same time. So when people see an actor onstage, they may be comparing her to someone else who has played that character. Think about it. Aren't there certain characters we can't picture anyone else playing? Good actors keep that in mind, but they do not let it intimidate them!

ONSTAGE STORYTELLING

Whether it's a *musical*, *comedy*, *drama*, or a combination of genres— and whether it is staged on Broadway, in a college auditorium, or a community theater—actors tell a story. Unlike television and movies, though, most plays do not have fancy special effects or computer-generated imagery (CGI) to depend on. Except for the scenery and *props*, it is up to

Theater actors often exaggerate their actions so that audiences can see everything. There's no camera to pick up smaller movements.

the actors to tell the story. Actors have to hit their marks, so they can tell the story of the play. And they have to convey action and the passage of time.

Because of the nature of a theater, acting in a play requires some special techniques. There is no physical barrier between the audience and those onstage. In most cases, they perform on an elevated stage in front of the audience. The audience has a clear view of the action onstage.

Actors need to remember to "play to the back row." That back row can be 100 feet from the stage! And those in the audience have to be able to hear and see what is happening onstage. Sometimes actors use microphones so those in the back can hear. But most of the time, those onstage must **project** their voices loudly enough to be heard by everyone in the theater.

Actions onstage have to be obvious enough they can be seen by those in the back. Actors exaggerate their motions, so they can be seen far away. But there is a fine line between exaggerating enough and exaggerating too much. Practice and study give actors the tools they need to provide the audience with a good theater experience.

LIGHTS! CAMERA! ACTION!

Acting on screen covers a lot of territory. There are opportunities to work on big-screen films and television programs. And like working in the theater, there are chances to work on dramas, musicals, comedies, and other genres.

Acting on the Screen

When considering a career in acting, many people automatically think of the big screen. What actor wouldn't want to see his image magnified to an almost unbelievable size? And then there are the fame and fortune that come with starring in a blockbuster film!

Here's a reality check, though: most films are *not* blockbuster hits. And most actors don't make a lot of money. Some have second jobs to make ends meet between film gigs.

For many years, actors who appeared in film wouldn't consider acting on television, even if they were unable to find film or stage roles. Some movie contracts actually forbade movie actors from appearing on television if they wanted to. For a lot of actors, appearing on television was considered beneath their abilities.

Make Connections

Broadway has the Tony Awards, and the film industry presents the Academy Award—the Oscar. The youngest person to receive the Oscar is Tatum O'Neal. She was 10 years, 148 days old when she won the award for Best Supporting Actress in 1974 for her role in *Paper Moon*.

Over the years, film actors have ventured onto the small screen, however. Cable networks, including HBO and Showtime, helped bring big-name stars to the small screen through high-quality movies and series.

Acting in Film

Many of the same skills needed to act in theater are also used when acting on film. Film performers need to be able to remember lines. They need to know how to hit their marks, so they and their fellow performers can be lit and seen properly. And they have to be able to tell a story through their acting.

There are some differences between acting on stage and the screen. In most films, scenes are not shot *sequentially*. For example, the director may decide to shoot all the film's nighttime scenes on one night. This may mean the ending is shot before the beginning. In the editing process, the film is then put together in the order you see on the screen.

Once a play begins, it continues until the curtain comes down at the end of the final act. Being a film actor or actress means a lot of starting and stopping … and waiting. You have to wait while a scene is shot that

Make Connections

Chroma keying takes two different videos and layers them on top one another. The actors perform in front of a green screen, and then another video showing movement in another scene is inserted into the background.

Computer-generated imaging allows live actors to appear to interact with various fantasy and science fiction creatures.

you are not in. You have to wait while a scene is set up. You have to wait while the director reviews a scene to see if it meets with her approval. Workdays can begin very early and run late. Or an actor may be called in to shoot just one scene and then go home.

Unlike plays, films can be shot on many locations. If a scene calls for mountains or oceans, the director can move the filming somewhere these occur naturally. There is no need to re-create the landscape indoors. The script doesn't need to be rewritten to avoid such natural features, which may help tell the story.

Sometimes things do not go as planned. Perhaps a line is flubbed or someone accidentally walks into a shot she's not supposed to be in. Or maybe the director decides it's not working the way he planned. If that happened during a play, changes would have to wait until the next performance. In film, the changes can be incorporated right away and the scene reshot. In editing, the unwanted scene is cut in favor of the new one.

An actor may sometimes be acting with an unseen costar. Through chroma keying, computer-generated imaging, and other postproduction

Research Project

The author says there was a time when film actors did not want or were not allowed to appear on television. Use the Internet and library to find one who did not want to appear on TV and one who chose to work in television. Write a paragraph on each, giving their reasons for making the decisions they made. Did they ever regret their decisions?

editing techniques, other actors—dinosaurs and aliens, for example—can be added to the scene.

Acting on Television

Many characteristics of acting on the big screen also apply to acting on television, especially for action dramas and made-for-television movies. Other programs are more like plays. Situation comedies and series that take place in just a few, mostly indoor locations are generally shot in sequence. There is often a live studio audience watching the final filming as well.

Television offers an acting opportunity not found in movies. Despite the label "reality series," many of these programs use actors to re-create scenes from real life. For example, a show that features an unsolved crime uses actors to show what led up to the crime and how it took place.

Unlike most films, where an actor plays a role once, some actors

Text-Dependent Questions

1. What options does the author present at the beginning of the chapter for those who want to act?
2. According to Paul Newman, what is acting?
3. According to the author, what does it mean to "play to the back row"?
4. How does acting in film differ from acting in plays?
5. Based on the material presented in the chapter, how can editing change a film?

have recurring roles in a television series. While filming a movie can mean being on set for many hours a day, filming a television series often has more traditional hours. There's a set time to start and a set time to end for the day. This can allow actors to have dinner and time with their families. Most shows also film for a few months and then go on vacation, called a hiatus. Those attached to the series can take time off with their families. They also have a chance to work on other projects.

Regardless of whether you aim for a career in the theater or on the screen, if you achieve your goal, you'll become part of acting's long history! You'll make stories come alive for viewers.

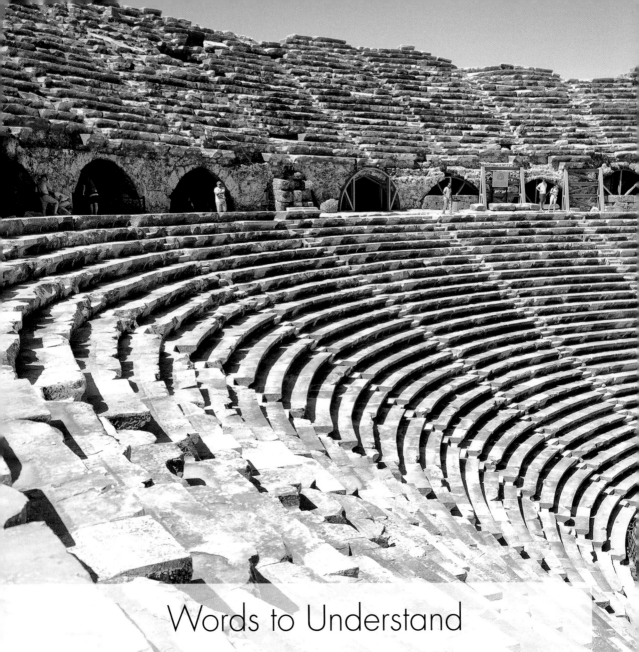

Words to Understand

therapy: Treatment to help someone with a disease or emotional problem.

hierarchy: An organization or society where people are ranked above and below each other.

classic: Universally recognized as being well-made and culturally significant.

Chapter Two

The History
of Acting on
Stage and Screen

Few careers have such a long history as acting. Most historians believe it can be traced back to Thespis, an actor in sixth-century BCE Greece. Though most of the earliest plays have been lost over time, some have survived. A few from ancient Greek playwrights, including Euripides and Sophocles, still exist. You won't find them performed often, but they do return to the stage from time to time.

Instead of taking place indoors, plays in ancient Greece usually took place in large outdoor theaters and stadiums. Crowds often numbered in the hundreds. Actors—who were only male performers—often wore heavily padded costumes. These costumes hid small movements, which

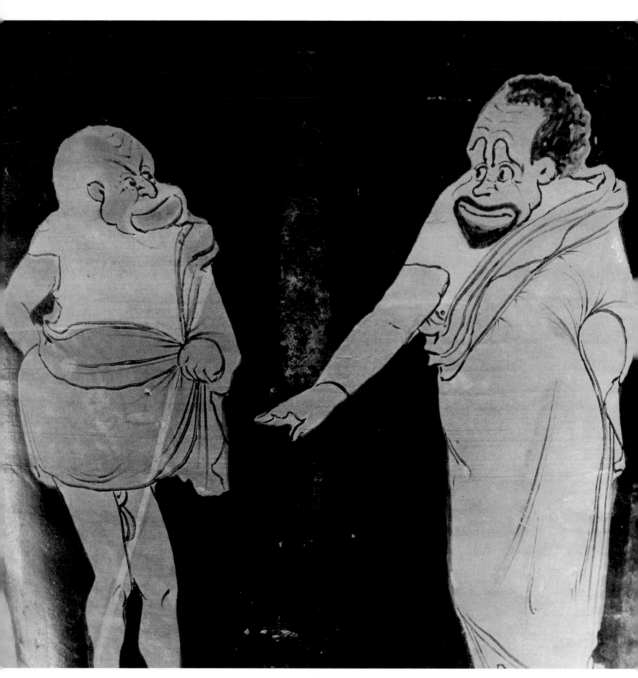

An image painted on Greek pottery shows two actors performing in a play that was viewed by audiences more than two thousand years ago.

Make Connections

Women slowly made their way to the stage outside England. While the English king Charles II lived in exile in Europe, he saw plays in which women played parts intended for females. After returning to England, he and other members of English society discussed allowing women onstage. The problem was how to do so without causing problems with his mostly Puritan subjects. His answer? He gave a charter to the Drury Lane Company, which became the Theatre Royal Company. King Charles II decided males dressing up to play female roles would upset the Puritans. So the charter declared that all female parts had to be played by females. The first woman to appear on the English stage because of the charter was Margaret Hughes. On December 8, 1660, she played Desdemona in *The Moor of Venice*.

were lost on the audience. Actors had to be bold in their movements in order to be seen.

Greek plays of the times were tragedies. They told stories of human suffering. One might think these plays would make audience members sad. Instead, they offered theatergoers an emotional release. After seeing such a play, audience members often felt better about their lives and the situations around them.

Acting eventually spread from Greece to Rome. During the Middle Ages in Rome, acting changed. While acting and plays had been almost like artful ***therapy*** in ancient Greece, they were much different in Rome. Acting now was considered to be more entertainment than an art form. Street performers—such as mimes, jugglers, and acrobats—were considered on the same level as actors. The Roman plays also told

The Globe Theatre as it would have appeared in Shakespeare's day. Today a reconstruction of the Globe has been built, and audiences can experience what it would have been like to attend a play in seventeenth-century England.

Make Connections

One of the best-known theaters in the world is the Globe Theatre. Constructed in 1599, the theater was designed for the Lord Chamberlain's Men, Shakespeare's theater company. Some believe Shakespeare wrote *As You Like It* to celebrate the Globe's opening. Shakespeare earned most of his income not from writing plays but from his share in the Globe.

different stories from those of ancient Greece. Plots revolving around human suffering were replaced by religion-based stories. And instead of being held in large, outdoor locations, plays were often performed in churches.

The next major development in acting occurred in England in the sixteenth and seventeenth centuries, especially in the works of William Shakespeare. He is perhaps the best-known playwright in the world. His plays continue to be performed today.

Today's theater companies may put on several performances of the same play a week. Members of theater companies during Shakespeare's time often put on six different plays in a week. But they were also expected to do many things besides act. They had to help build sets and props. And they were responsible for making costumes. The lower you were on the company's ladder, the more nonacting tasks you had. Boys were at the bottom of the company *hierarchy* and were responsible for the doing the lowliest tasks. But they could earn some stage time. Since women were still not allowed to perform onstage—acting was not considered a suitable occupation for women—young boys usually filled female roles.

We usually think of Charlie Chaplin with his trademark hat and mustache—but this is what the actor looked like under the makeup and costume.

BECOMING PROFESSIONAL

Acting was not really taken seriously for many years. It was considered more of a hobby than a career, or at least not a career to be taken seriously. Many people outside the theater considered it an unseemly profession and looked down on actors and those associated with the profession. But a new style of acting began changing people's opinions.

In its early history, actors often stood still and spoke loudly, often gesturing wildly. In some cases, like the padded costumes mentioned earlier, this was necessary. But as costumes became easier to wear, there was still the tendency to yell, slam doors, and throw things. Today, it would likely be said they were overacting.

Early in the twentieth century, acting techniques began to change. Actors—male and female—wanted to appear more natural in their performances. They wanted to do more than play the character as written in the play. Actors wanted to identify with the characters, to "get into their heads." Actors believed this would allow them to give a more accurate and more in-depth portrayal of characters.

Russian director Konstantin Stanislavski developed one of the best-known acting methods. Called the Stanislavski method, many actors have learned and used it to develop a more natural acting style. Though often taught first as a stage technique, screen actors can use the technique as well.

THE HISTORY OF SCREEN ACTING

Acting changed in the early 1900s with films. Though film had been around for over a decade, it wasn't until the turn of the century that what most people consider true movies developed. These movies were longer than most of the films that had been shown before. Techniques such as editing now were used.

The first movies were silent, usually one-reel shorts. Charlie Chaplin was the best-known actor of the early 1900s. His film *The Tramp* is

Clara Bow was one of the first celebrity movie stars.

considered a *classic*. After it was released, Chaplin's popularity meant he could ask for a high salary—but no one in the young film industry could afford to pay him as much as he wanted. Rather than settle for making less money, beginning in the 1920s, Chaplin only appeared in movies he also produced. *The Kid* is one of those movies.

Sound was added to film in 1929, and the 1930s became known as the Golden Age of Hollywood. Some in the movie industry, like Charlie Chaplin, did not like that development. Several stars of the silent era had difficulty making the transition to sound films. Clara Bow, the "It Girl," for example, was a big silent movie star, but when sound came, she had a hard time making the crossover. A thick accent wasn't a big deal in silent films, but it was a major obstacle to overcome when it came to sound. After a while, though, Clara was able to make the move to "talkies." Many others weren't.

Filmmaking slowed during the Depression and World War II. Producers didn't have as much money to invest in making film, many actors were busy with the war, and ordinary people had less money for going to the movies. By the end of the 1940s, however, filmmaking was thriving again. Actors who had left the business to fight in the war returned to their careers. And newcomers like Humphrey Bogart were ready to become part of the film scene.

Television became another acting opportunity in the 1950s, and as television became increasingly popular, actors made their way onto television. The first was Charlton Heston. Western film star Gene Autry was the first movie star to have a television series. Today, we often see stars we love on television appear in a movie. And those we love to watch on the big screen show up in our homes on a television show.

AN ACTING DYNASTY

Sometimes members of the same family end up in the same career—and the same is true in acting. But the Barrymore family is unique in what they have given to acting.

Research Project

The author mentions the Stanislavski acting method. Use the Internet or library to research other acting techniques. Make a list their main characteristics and how they are similar to and different from the Stanislavski method. Include a list of actors who studied these methods.

The first in long line of acting Barrymores was Herbert Blythe. He came to the United States in 1874 to become an actor. Under the stage name Maurice Barrymore, he became a Broadway actor.

Maurice and his wife, Georgiana Drew, had three children: Lionel, Ethel, and John. They all became actors. Ethel's films include *The Spiral Staircase* and *The Portrait of Jennie*. Both are often shown on television. Lionel's movies include the Christmas classic *It's a Wonderful Life*, in which he stars as the hated Mr. Potter. He's also well known for his portrayal of loveable characters, such as Dr. Gillespie in the *Dr. Kildare* movies and as the loving grandfather with death trapped in a tree in the film *On Borrowed Time*.

John is the least famous of the Barrymore siblings. He is perhaps best known as an alcoholic and the grandfather of actress, producer, and director Drew Barrymore. He appeared as a washed-up silent screen star in the film *Dinner at Eight*. His son, John Blyth Barrymore (who later changed his name to John Drew Barrymore), appeared in many television series. Among them were *Rawhide* and *Gunsmoke*. Unfortunately, addiction to alcohol and physical and mental conditions cut short his career.

Text-Dependent Questions

1. How does the author describe Greek theater at the beginning of the chapter?
2. According to the author, what are some ways Roman theater differed from Greek theater?
3. Long ago, why were women not allowed to act on stage? What changed that in England?
4. The author says silent screen star Charlie Chaplin eventually turned to acting only in movies he produced. Why?
5. This chapter indicates that some silent stars had difficulty transitioning to talkies. Why did Clara Bow have a problem finding success in sound pictures at first?

John Drew Barrymore's daughter Drew now represents the Barrymore acting dynasty. She entered the family profession early. Though she'd appeared in other films, Drew came to the attention of critics and public alike with her appearance in 1982's *E. T.* as Elliott's sister, Gertie. She had substance abuse issues when she was a teenager, but Drew worked through them. Though she still acts, Drew has expanded into producing and directing as well.

When it comes to the world of acting, the Barrymore family is an inspiration. Watch some of their work. See what you can learn!

Words to Understand

grants: Money given by an organization such as the government to do something specific.

scholarships: Money given to students to help them pay for an education.

internships: Training positions that help young people gain work experience.

stipend: A certain amount of money paid to do a job, usually just enough to cover basic living expenses.

agents: People who represent an actor and find them work.

casting: The process of finding actors to play the parts in a movie or play.

veteran: Someone who has been doing something for a long time and has lots of experience.

auditioned: Tried out for an acting role.

union: A group of workers in the same industry that work together to fight for better rights and treatment.

negotiates: Tries to reach an agreement or compromise.

publicity: The attention given to someone by the media.

HOLLYWOOD

PRODUCTION_____

DIRECTOR_____

CAMERA_____

DATE   SCENE   TAKE

Chapter Three

The Business of Acting on Stage and Screen

Acting is an art. It takes great skill to become a good actor—but it's also a business that earns money for many people.

People who decide to go into acting as a career often do not think about the business side. Their thoughts are often focused on fame, fortune, and potential projects. Who wouldn't be fascinated by the idea of his name above the title on the movie marquee?

Like all life decisions, choosing a career takes more than daydreaming; it requires serious planning. In most businesses, you will have to spend money to reach your goal. Yes, others will pay you to act in their projects, but that may be a long time in the future, and it may not be as much as you expected. Most actors will be responsible for their acting-related expenses for some time.

Acting has changed a lot since the days of Roman theater, shown here in a mosaic from more than two thousand years ago. But like today's stock companies, Roman theater had a limited cast and used stock characters.

CLASSES

You may be like many people who decide to become actors after taking an acting class or being involved in drama in high school. Most go on to college, and some study to fulfill their goals of becoming actors. Your college education can be considered one of your first acting expenses.

What Are Stock Companies?

Stock companies have existed in the United States since the 1880s. Summer stock companies perform in the summer (hence the "summer" in their names). Performances are frequently held outside in the afternoon or early evening. Though they aren't as common as they once were, some still perform and can provide young actors with valuable experience. Many consist of a limited cast, enough actors to play a hero, villain, heroine, and a younger male and a younger female character. Sets, props, and costumes are taken from what the company has in "stock" from other seasons. They often put on different plays during the season. Sometimes they perform a variety of plays in a week. That's a lot of work!

Parents often pay many of their children's college expenses. Look for *grants*, *scholarships*, and loans to help cover other expenses. You can also look find a part-time job. Keep in mind, though, that you'll need time for rehearsals and performances should you be cast in a production. Not all employers will want to adjust work schedules around performances. Be prepared with other options.

Summer vacations are good opportunities for many students to earn money for college. Lucky ones can find jobs or *internships* related to their chosen careers. Some summer stock companies offer opportunities for budding actors. Many are unpaid, but some offer a *stipend*. Not all will be acting positions, but you will have the opportunity to learn about acting and the theater.

Once you're out of school, classes should not end. Most actors continue taking classes for many years. Acting classes help hone skills and

Richard Dreyfuss believes that acting classes helped him make the award-winning actor he is today.

keep them up to date and fresh. Oscar-winning actor Richard Dreyfuss has talked about the opportunities classes provide.

> When I got my Academy Award, I thought it was a goal best kept in front of me. I liked the pursuit more than the arrival. I'm much better when I'm hungry. Act more hours of the day than not. Act for free. And if you're lucky, every once in a while, you'll get paid. Classes give you the opportunity to act. The more you act, the better you get. So go out and act. Pay for the privilege. Or are you going to wait until some director tells you to do something and you don't know how to deal with it? So you go to class to practice that, and to be filled with the enthusiasm for acting.

Acting classes can also teach you things that might not have been covered in college courses. For example, perhaps your school didn't have many classes in stage combat. You may want to take the class to learn to fight but also to learn more about moving onstage. Or maybe your school only had classes for acting in the theater, and you want to be in movies. There are classes available just for that.

Many actors also take dance classes. Again, some do so to be able to add dance to their skill set. Others take dance to improve their movements onstage or in film. Singing classes can be a good option if you want to be eligible for parts in a musical.

Though technically not acting classes, actors also often take exercise or yoga classes. Acting is a stressful career mentally and physically. Regular exercise and yoga techniques can calm the body and mind, as well as keep actors in good physical shape.

Classes are an expensive investment. The costs vary, and so does what you can expect from the classes. Acting classes can run from hundreds to thousands of dollars for a session. When considering a class, do your homework beforehand. Find out as much as you can about the

Actor Susan Sullivan believes that acting is both a career and a craft—an art form with techniques that must be continually improved.

Make Connections

Susan Sullivan, Emmy and Golden Globe nominee, and star of *Castle*, has this to say about being an actor:

The great adventure of being an actor is that acting is a continuing education. As an adjunct to whatever your career might be, you should continue working on your craft. The great joy of acting is to be an artist, and that requires intelligence, commitment, and depth. The good news is that I have to get up in the morning and create my day. The bad news is that I have to get up in the morning and create my day.

class and the teacher. Whenever possible, talk to students who have taken the class. That way you can be sure you'll get your money's worth.

THE PORTFOLIO

Every actor needs a portfolio. A portfolio is an organized collection of photographs and other information directors, **agents**, and other professionals can refer to when making decisions about callbacks and **casting**.

High-quality head shots are necessary for all actors. Early in their careers, some actors use a friend to take their head shots. Professionally taken photographs can be very expensive. There's no problem having a friend take the photographs—as long as he is a good photographer. After you get an agent, she will likely help you find a professional photographer to take better portraits.

Make certain your contact information is printed on the photographs. Clipped pieces of paper with such information can too easily become separated from the photo.

Lots of people have big dreams—but it takes hard work to make dreams come true.

Along with the head shots and other photographs, a résumé is included in the portfolio. This has the usual items included in a résumé, as well as information about roles, acting-related classes, and other training should be provided.

THE AGENT

While actors can live without a publicist and personal assistant when just starting out, most need an agent. Agents help them find roles to audition for.

Some agents specialize in a particular medium. Theatrical agents represent actors on the stage. Other agents represent clients who want

Make Connections

Most auditions are closed. You—or more likely your agent—have to make an appointment if you want to try out for a part. Some auditions, though, are open. Also sometimes called "cattle calls," these auditions are open to anyone who comes to a specified place to audition. These auditions are often very crowded, so be sure to come prepared with something to do while you wait your turn. It could be hours of waiting!

to be in movies. Television and commercial actors have their own specialist agents. And there are agents whose clients are in all forms of acting.

Paying for an agent isn't like paying for someone to teach you something or take your photographs. An agent works for a percentage of what the actors receive for a job gotten through the agent. On average, an agent takes 10 to 15 percent of what the client is paid.

Because agents get paid on a percentage basis, they need to be fairly certain their clients can get roles on a regular basis. An agent may want to help a new actor, but if she isn't convinced she will be able to him acting jobs, she won't make money. And after all, she's in business to make money. Because of the risk agents take when accepting clients, they tend not to take on too many new ones. Their "stables" are usually made up of several **veteran** actors and a few new ones. To increase your chances of getting an agent—and one who has good contacts in the field—get as much acting experience as possible. Agents want to know you have worked in the field, regularly **auditioned** for roles and gotten them, and have a good reputation. Be sure to save any positive reviews your performances receive.

DUES

Although it isn't always necessary to belong to a **union**, most actors do. Unions can help assure actors are paid what they deserve and are treated well. There are two main unions for actors.

Actors Equity Association (Equity) **negotiates** with producers on working conditions for stage actors. If you want to appear in a Broadway play or perform in one of the small Equity theaters around the country, you will need to join Equity. The union allows a small number of nonmembers to work in Equity plays. After performing in a specified number of plays, the actor is allowed to join Equity. For up-to-date requirements for joining this union, visit Actors Equity's website: actorsequity.org.

The other union is the Screen Actors Guild–American Federation of Television & Radio Artists (SAG-AFTRA). This union is for actors who make films or appear on television and radio. SAG-AFTRA only involves performances that are filmed. If performances are only videotaped, SAG-AFTRA membership is not required. To become eligible for membership, one of the following conditions must be met.

1. Proof of SAG or AFTRA employment
2. Employment under an affiliated performers' union

For complete requirements, check out the organization's website: www.sagaftra.org.

Union membership can be beneficial, but there are rules to follow. Perhaps the most important one is that once you belong to a union, you cannot work for a nonunion project.

PUBLICIST AND PERSONAL ASSISTANT

You often hear about an actor's publicist or personal assistant. For most actors, these positions can be filled after getting established. So what do they do?

In short, they pretty much do what the titles suggest. A publicist helps

Make Connections

It can be difficult to find an agent. Agents assume a lot of risk when taking on new clients, so their reluctance to add to their client base can be understood. You might be so anxious to sign with an agent that you're tempted to sign up with anyone who offers to represent you. Do your homework first. Ask for a list of clients, and contact some of them. Have they been pleased with the proposed agent's services? Has the agent found them acting jobs? Is the agent respectful of the client and his parents? And keep this in mind. If the agent asks for money in advance, say, "Thank you," and walk away.

her client get *publicity*—hopefully positive publicity. When the actor participates in a project, she makes sure the press knows about it. If the actor becomes involved in a charity, she makes sure they know that, too. And she's there to handle the press should the actor get involved in something not so positive. In those cases, however, a crisis specialist may be called in.

Hiring a publicist can be very expensive. In some cases, especially when actors are starting out, a publicist may work for more than one client. This way, the fee can be shared.

Acting can be time-consuming, especially as one becomes more established. A personal assistant can take care of everyday chores such as shopping, laundry, and the like. He can also handle fan mail and the actor's Web page or blog.

PAYING FOR IT

Now that you know some of the costs involved in the business of acting, how can you pay for them while you're waiting for your first big break?

Research Project

According to the information presented in this chapter, many actors start out by working more than one job to support themselves. Pick one of your favorite actors and use the Internet or the library to find out more about the story of his or her career. What jobs did this person work at the beginning of his or her career? What was this actor's first big break? How old was this person before acting became his or her primary means of support? How much money does this person make now?

Many actors work at other jobs as well when they're starting out. Or they may take advantage of smaller acting opportunities. Training films need actors, for example, as do films promoting products and places. These aren't exactly art, but they do pay actors for their work.

Sometimes actors can have long and successful careers without being seen. Voiceover actors make cartoon characters and other animated characters speak. They also provide the unseen voices on television and radio commercials. They act as narrators for documentaries.

Actors are also used in computer games and video games where their bodies are scanned and turned into virtual characters. Like television series, computer and video games can lead to long-term acting gigs.

Here are some other ideas for ways you can get paid for your acting skills:

- Coach younger or less-experienced actors. Help them rehearse a role or prepare for an audition. They often can't pay a lot, but every little bit helps.

Text-Dependent Questions

1. What reasons does the author give for taking classes?
2. What suggestions does the author make for paying for classes?
3. According to this chapter, what should be included in an actor's portfolio?
4. How are agents paid?
5. What opportunities are available for voiceover actors?

- Teach or help teach classes or workshops. Not only will you help someone develop as an actor, you'll learn more about your art.
- If you have writing skills, consider writing about acting. You don't have to write the complete book of acting or an all-inclusive history of acting. An article, blog post, or newsletter can help others find their ways in the acting world. It can also earn you some money and get your name out to the acting world.

As you think about whether to become an actor, remember the financial costs involved. If acting is what you really want to do, you will find a way!

Words to Understand

syndicated: Broadcast on a number of different television stations, instead of just one.

Chapter Four

How Can I Get Involved in Acting?

So you think you want to be an actor. At least you are interested in it now, and you want to give it a try. But you are not quite sure how to get involved.

The simple and easiest answer is to act. Seriously. You will never know if acting is something you like to do unless you do it. And there are more opportunities than you might think.

SCHOOLS

Many schools have acting clubs. Get involved. Not only can you learn about acting and have opportunities to act, but you will also have the

Community actors may put on open-air performances at summer events.

chance to get involved with other aspects of theater. It takes a lot to put on a play or make a film. The actors are just a part. You also learn about how to create a set, how to manage a stage, and how to do the lighting and sound control. You could learn about how to advertise a play by creating posters and websites. You might learn about how to create costumes or do makeup for a performance.

Even if your school does not have a theater group, other schools in your area may. Some schools will let students from other schools audition for their plays. It does not hurt to check.

Also pay attention to plays colleges and universities are putting on in your area. A play may call for someone younger than the students at the college. They may be looking for someone just like you for the role.

CLUBS AND ORGANIZATIONS

The Boys and Girls Clubs, scouts, and other organizations often put on plays. They provide more opportunities to act and get involved with other parts of play production. It also gives you the opportunity to perform in front of people who may not have seen you act before. This can help build your confidence. As you progress in your acting, you will have to audition and perform in front of larger groups of strangers. Doing it now will help you prepare for the future.

COMMUNITY THEATER

Most cities have community theaters. Some community theaters put on one play a season. Others perform multiple plays in multiple genres. Performances are generally at night, though there are often weekend matinees. Because most cast members probably have jobs and family responsibilities, hours required for rehearsals and performances are not too overwhelming for younger actors.

Performing with community theaters can also expose you to material you might otherwise not become aware of until years later. Schools and young people's organization tend to put on plays geared for a

If you want to be a professional actor, you should consider auditioning for commercials. Starting out at the local level is a way to gain experience while earning some money.

Make Connections: Stagecraft

Putting on a play or making a film requires more than actors. "Stagecraft" is the term used to describe the technical aspects of production. It includes working with scenery and lighting, designing and making costumes, handling props, and doing makeup and hair.

young audience. Although there may be a special performance of a play aimed at a younger audience, a community theater tends to produce more mature plays. Even so, most are aimed at a family audience, especially those with roles for young actors. Everything you learn about putting on a play helps your acting.

COMMERCIALS

Most cities have at least one advertising agency. They may be able to provide you with information about getting into commercials. Many young actors began in commercials. They provide acting opportunities and, of course, a paycheck. Perhaps most important, commercials—even ones for local businesses—can provide lots of exposure. Think about how many times a day you see a commercial for a local business. Now imagine you in a few of those!

The more your work is seen, the greater your chance of being hired for another commercial and another. Commercial makers from outside your immediate area may see your commercials, and you could be offered opportunities to make commercials for businesses in other locations. Eventually, your work could come to the attention of national businesses. And if they know about you, you can be selected for a national

Being a news announcer could give you important experience, helping you be more comfortable in front of a camera, while teaching you to communicate clearly with your voice.

Make Connections

Actors have the chance to explore other aspects of their personalities. In a way, they get paid for playing make-believe! According to Leonardo DiCaprio, "The best thing about acting is that I get to lose myself in another character and actually get paid for it ... It's a great outlet. I'm not really sure who I am—it seems I change every day."

campaign. All that would not have happened had you not contacted your local commercial company. Besides, you will have some film to add to your portfolio when searching for other acting opportunities.

LOCAL NEWS AND KIDS' PROGRAMMING

Local television stations have a certain number of broadcast hours devoted to children's programming. Many of these are national or **syndicated** programs. But some stations produce programs aimed at young people in their communities.

Other stations create news broadcasts for young people. Most stories deal with local events and activities of interest to the community's younger members. A young reporter may bring watchers the story of a new birth at the zoo, results of local sports teams, and details of a read-a-thon at the library. There might be an interview with the mayor about how new mall hours will affect teen moviegoers.

The broadcasts are by and for a young audience. While not acting per se, they provide you with time in front of the camera. In most places, it is easier to get stage experience than film or video. This type

Being a fashion model could be a place for you to get a start. Some celebrity actors started out as models.

Maybe one day this will be your license plate!

of programming gives you that experience. And again, you will have some film or video to add to your acting portfolio.

MODELING

Modeling might seem like an odd suggestion for someone who wants to be an actor. But what is modeling except performing? If you're modeling in a runway show, you will gain experience in appearing in front of

Don't be afraid to try out for a role! The more you audition, the more comfortable you will be the next time, even if you don't get the role this time.

Casting directors often have something in mind when it comes to a particular role. It could just be you!

a live audience. If you're doing a catalog shoot or newspaper ad, you gain skills in working in front of a camera. Regardless of the type of modeling, you'll sharpen skills that can help your acting.

REGIONAL AND NATIONAL SEARCHES

Sometimes you may hear a story on the news about a countrywide search for an actor to play a particular role. These are often calls for young actors. Casting directors or others connected with the project travel the country, holding auditions in towns and cities. If those affiliated with the project are coming to your area, your local news will likely have stories about it on television and radio, as well as in the newspaper.

If you use the Internet to find out where and when auditions will be held, you'll know exactly where to go for casting calls.

Research Project

This chapter discusses different avenues you can take to find opportunities to act. Using the suggestions provided by the author, make a list of acting options available in your area. Include the type of productions done by each option. Add contact information if you can find it. Do you see anything you might consider auditioning for?

But what if they are not coming to your city? How can you get details? The Internet, of course! Just because you live far from areas usually associated with theater and filmmaking does not mean you can only perform there. Thanks to the Internet, you can find information about auditions almost anywhere in the world.

Using your favorite search engine, type in "open auditions," "casting calls," or "open calls." Up will come lists of projects holding auditions, divided into geographic areas. Though you can easily find references to casting being done in New York City or Hollywood, there will sometimes be listings for other locations too. Check the listings regularly. Additions are often made without notice, and you want to be sure you know what is available.

Whether you go to a closed or open audition, be sure to take any materials asked for in the notice. If they want head shots or other photographs, check to see they are in your portfolio. The same with a résumé. And make sure your résumé includes your most recent performances.

To become an actor, especially a good one, you have to act. And without acting experience, it may be difficult to find the chance to do just that. Take every opportunity to gain experience in the theater or in front

Text-Dependent Questions

1. What suggestions does the author make as possible acting opportunities available to young people?
2. What are three things that fall under the label of "stagecraft"?
3. The author discusses ways commercials can help your acting career. List them.
4. What subjects are likely to be covered in a newscast aimed at young viewers?
5. What is the difference between open auditions (open calls) and closed auditions (closed calls)?

of a camera. Everything you learn about theater and film—even things not directly related to acting—adds knowledge you can draw from for a performance.

The more you act, the more people in the business will see and become familiar with your work. The chances increase of being asked to audition for a project. And who knows where that could lead!

Find Out More

Online

Actor 101
www.backstage.com/actor101

Industry Tips: The Ins and Outs of the Acting Business
www.sft.edu/tips/tips.html

So You Want to Be an Actor?
www.forbes.com/sites.alexandratalty.2013/11/21/so-you-want-to-be-an-actor

So You Want to Be an Actor? How to Begin a Career in Acting and Find Auditions
www.tvdramas.about.com/od/actingresources/a/becomeanactor.htm

TheatrGroup
www.theatrgroup.com/showbiz

In Books

Belli, Mary Lou, and Dinah Lenney. *Acting for Young Actors: The Ultimate Teen Guide.* New York: Back Stage Books, 2006.

Levy, Gavin. 275 *Acting Games: Connected—A Comprehensive Workbook of Theatre Games for Developing Acting Skills.* Colorado Springs, Colo.: Meriwether, 2010.

Russell, Paul. *Acting: Make It Your Business—How to Avoid Mistakes and Achieve Success as a Working Actor.* New York: Back Stage Books, 2008.

Shurtleff, Michael. *Audition: Everything an Actor Needs to Get the Part.* New York: Walker and Company, 2013.

Sudol, John. *Acting Face to Face: An Actor's Guide to Understand How Your Face Communicates Emotion for TV and Film.* New York: CreateSpace Independent Publishing Platform, 2013.

Series Glossary of Key Terms

Abstract: Made up of shapes that are symbolic. You might not be able to tell what a piece of abstract art is just by looking at it.

Classical: A certain kind of art traditional to the ancient Greek and Roman civilizations. In music, it refers to music in a European tradition that includes opera and symphony and that is generally considered more serious than other kinds of music.

Culture: All the arts, social meanings, thoughts, and behaviors that are common in a certain country or group.

Gallery: A room or a building that displays art.

Genre: A category of art, all with similar characteristics or styles.

Impressionism: A style of painting that focuses more on the artist's perception of movement and lighting than what something actually looks like.

Improvisation: Created without planning or preparation.

Medium (media): The materials or techniques used to create a work of art. Oil paints are a medium. So is digital photography.

Pitch: How high or low a musical note is; where it falls on a scale.

Portfolio: A collection of some of the art an artist has created, to show off her talents.

Realism: Art that tries to show something exactly as it appears in real life.

Renaissance: A period of rapid artistic and literary development during the 1500s–1700s, or the name of the artistic style from this period.

Studio: A place where an artist can work and create his art.

Style: A certain way of creating art specific to a person or time period.

Technique: A certain way of creating a piece of art.

Tempo: How fast a piece of music goes.

Venue: The location or facility where an event takes place.

Index

Academy Awards (Oscars) 14, 35
Actors Equity Association (Equity) 40
agent 37–39, 41
American Theatre Wing (Tony Awards)
    11, 14
audition 38–39, 42, 47, 54–58

Barrymore family 27–29
Bogart, Humphrey 27
Bow, Clara 26–27, 29
Broadway 11, 14, 28, 40

"cattle calls" 39
Chaplin, Charlie 24–25, 27, 29
chroma keying 15
classes 11, 32–35, 38, 43
comedy 11
commercials 39, 42, 48–49, 51, 58
community theater 9, 11, 47, 49
computer-generated imagery (CGI) 11

Dinner at Eight 28
Dr. Kildare 28
drama 11, 13, 16, 32
Drew, Georgiana 28–29

E. T. 29
editing 8, 14–17, 25

filmmaking 27, 57
film/movies 8, 11, 13–17, 25–31, 35,
    39–40, 42, 47, 49, 51, 53, 58

Globe Theatre 22–23
Golden Age of Hollywood 27
Greek theater 29

Gunsmoke 28

head shots 37–38, 57

It's a Wonderful Life 28

The Kid 27
kids' programming 51

Michaels, Frankie 11
modeling 53, 55
musical 11, 13, 35

O'Neal, Tatum 14
On Borrowed Time 28

personal assistant 38, 40–41
playwright 9–11, 19, 23
plot 23
portfolio 37–38, 43, 51, 53, 57
The Portrait of Jennie 28
publicist 38, 40–41
publicity 30, 41
Puritans 21

Rawhide 28
reality series 16
résumé 38, 57
Roman theater 29, 32
royalty 9

school play 9
Screen Actors Guild–American Fed-
    eration of Television & Radio Artists
    (SAG-AFTRA) 40
searches (regional or national) 55

Shakespeare, William 10–11, 22–23
short 9, 25, 28, 40
situation comedy 16
The Spiral Staircase 28
stagecraft 49, 58
Stanislavski, Konstantin 25, 28
stock companies 32–33
summer stock 33

television 8, 11, 13, 16–17, 27–28,
    39–40, 42, 44, 51, 55

theater companies 9, 23
theater (theatre) 8–9, 11–14, 17, 21–23,
    25, 29, 32–33, 35, 47, 49, 57–58
Thespis 19
tragedies 21
The Tramp 25

union 30, 40

About the Author

Z.B. Hill is a an author, actor, and publicist living in Binghamton, New York. He has a special interest in education and how art can be used in the classroom.

Picture Credits

Fotolia.com:
6: Ljupco Smokovski
12: Николай Григорьев
18: Antony McAulay
30: Elnur
38: Serg Nvns
50: redav
52: Jason Stitt

Dreamstime.com:
34: David Fowler
36: Sbukley

44: Oleg Tovkach
46: Sindorei
48: Daniel Raustadt
53: Stephen Coburn
54: Innovatedcaptures
55: Alexander Mitrofanov
56: Seandeburca

20: Louvre Museum
24: National Media Museum
26: Library of Congress
32: Marie-Lan Nguyen